EXPLAINING
ADDICTION
For Kids

By Tracy Bryan

Drug: something that is used to change how a person is feeling.

EXPLAINING
ADDICTION

For Kids

By Tracy Bryan

Most kids have a favorite food that they like to eat.

Do you? Could you eat this food everyday?

That might get a little boring, don't you think?

What if it was CANDY or CHOCOLATE?

Could you eat these foods for every meal?

Of course not!

You might want to eat candy or chocolate everyday, but eventually these foods would make you really sick if you ate them that much.

Candy and chocolate are treat foods- they are food that we should have in moderation.

What is MODERATION? Food moderation is eating something in a healthy way, every once in a while, because it's special.

Too many treat foods make us sick, because they have ingredients in them that cause unhealthy effects to our body and brain, if we have too much of them.

One ingredient that treat foods usually have in them is SUGAR.

In small amounts, sugar isn't harmful to our bodies. If we eat a lot of sugar in our foods though, it can make us sick.

Kids between the ages of 4-8 should have about 12.5 g per day. Just one 12-ounce serving of most soda (one can) contains about 39 grams of sugar. (1) Yikes!

Sometimes we eat sugary treat foods because of a special occasion; like a birthday party or a family outing. That's okay to do every once in a while, but most days it's healthiest for our body to eat sugar in moderation.

There are some things in our life that we should probably DO in moderation too.

Are there fun activities that you really love to do?

Playing video games, watching television, creating art, doing a sport or a hobby?

It's important to have fun activities to do-everyone needs to have some fun in their life.

Unfortunately, we can't ALWAYS do fun things.

Even if we WANT to, we cant just do activities that are fun. Sometimes we NEED to do activities that keep us healthy too.

We need to do things to keep our body healthy- like brushing our teeth and hair, bathing, going to the bathroom and dressing.

We also need to do activities to keep our brain healthy- like going to school, reading and spending time with our family.

Having moderation in our day balances everything, so we have a healthy BODY and BRAIN.

Not too much and not too little. Moderation is all about eating and doing just enough.

Just enough to fill us up with a whole bunch of different foods...but, not over fill us and make our body sick from giving it too many treat foods.

Just enough of each activity...but, not making our body exhausted from doing too much of just one thing.

Adults have treats too. Some adults eat treat foods.

These foods may be the same as treats for kids; like chocolate and candy. Adults can digest these better than kids though because their body systems are more developed than a kid's body is.

Adults also don't usually feel as sick as kids do when they eat too many treat foods, because they are more used to eating them. Their body is already grown and doesn't react to sugar as much as a kid's growing body does.

There are many adults that can get really sick from treat foods too. These adults usually have to take special medication because their body cant have a lot of sugar. They are DIABETIC.

Most people (adults and kids) eat a lot more sugar than they should. A lot of the foods that we buy or order in a restaurant are filled with extra sugar.

To be healthy, it's important to read FOOD LABELS if you can, to see how much sugar is in the food that you eat.

Some adults drink "treat drinks."
COFFEE and TEA are treat drinks. Kids shouldn't have these because they have caffeine in them.

CAFFEINE is a drug- it makes adults feel more awake and alert.

A DRUG is something that is used to change how a person is feeling. It also affects what they say and do. Most drugs are like treats for adults-they should be used in moderation.

There are certain drugs that an adult (and child) must take if they have an illness or if they are just temporarily sick. These drugs, if taken in the right amount, are healthy for us. These kinds of drugs are usually PRESCRIPTION MEDICATION that we get from the doctor.

Other drugs that adults might use or take are CIGARETTES and ALCOHOL.

Some adults might smoke cigarettes. Smoking a lot or for a long time is really harmful to their health, so they will have to quit eventually. Also, hopefully they don't smoke around kids and people that don't smoke.

Some adults might drink a little bit of alcohol, and as long as they use moderation, this won't harm their body.

Some adults might even use ILLEGAL DRUGS. These are drugs that the government doesn't allow people to buy or use. These kinds of drugs can make a person really sick.

Any drug that is used for a long time can harm a person's body and brain. This is called addiction.

ADDICTION is when a person's body becomes dependent on a drug. They start to crave that drug and want to use it all the time.

Adults can become addicted to cigarettes, alcohol and illegal drugs. When someone uses any drug in a harmful way, it is called DRUG ABUSE. Abusing drugs too much leads to addiction.

Addiction is very common. When people use drugs, it's usually because they want to feel better.

Drugs don't make us feel better though, and some people don't understand this-even adults.

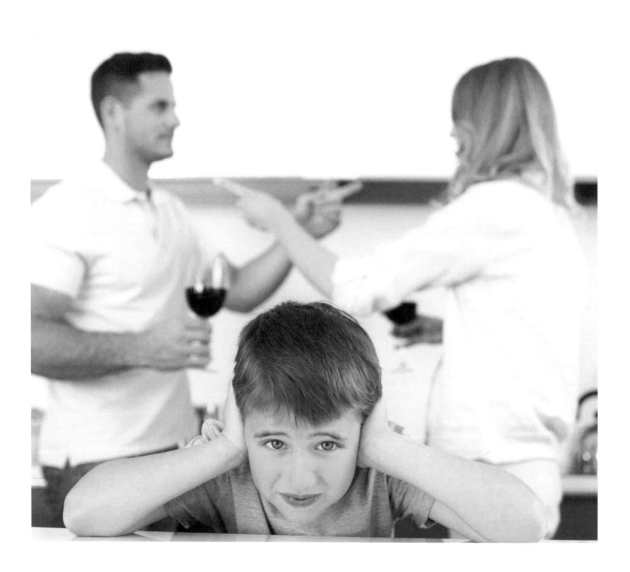

Some adults keep abusing a drug to feel better, until they get addicted to it.

People who have addictions need to get help.

Living with someone who has an addiction can be really difficult too, because usually this person changes a little. They are so focused on getting and using the drug they are addicted to, they sometimes forget about the important people in their life.

People who are addicted to a drug get irritable, angry and scared- they fear they won't be able to have what they want, so they get panicky and mad.

People who are addicted to something have problems with the way their body works unless they stop their addiction.

With help from professionals, people who are addicted to a drug can get treatment for their brain and body. This can be a very long recovery process, but there are many treatment programs available for anyone with an addiction.

If you know someone who has an addiction, the best thing that you can do is have HOPE.

Also, remember that this is their problem, it has NOTHING TO DO WITH YOU.

Most of all, to help them, just give them lots of LOVE!

Glossary

abuse-to use wrongly or improperly, misuse

addiction-when a person's body becomes dependent on a drug

caffeine- a drug that makes adults feel more awake and alert

compulsive - a need to behave over and over

drug-something that is used to change how a person is feeling

moderation- avoidance of extremes or excesses

excess- more than or above what is necessary or usual

extreme-beyond moderation

function- the purpose for something

prescribed- an order for the use of

stimulant-something that temporarily quickens a body function

substance- physical matter or material, could be chemical

Worry Meditation

When someone we love has an addiction, it's difficult not to worry about them. We want them to feel better and help them recover from their addiction. Try this worry meditation. Find a quiet space and do it everyday if you want. It will help make your worries go away so you can focus on being strong and loving to the person that needs it-especially yourself! You can have a trusted adult or friend read it for you. You may even want to read it aloud to yourself. When the addicted person you love is feeling better, they might just want to do it with you!

You are lying in a boat. The sun feels warm on your body and the ocean waves gently rock you. You hear the birds above you and the odd splash of water as it meets the boat.

In the distance you hear a humming sound.

It's another boat coming to see you. The driver is a kind old woman.

She pulls up next to your boat and says she has brought the bye bye boat for you.

First she asks for your worries. You gather them all up and put them onto her boat.

Then she asks for your anger. You gather it all up and put it onto her boat too.

Finally she asks for your fear - all that you are frightened of. You collect all your fear and put that on the bye bye boat too.

She smiles at you, and you smile back, feeling so good now you don't have to carry all the worries, anger and fear any more.

She starts the engine, gives a little wave and drives the bye bye boat away.

You open your eyes and feel refreshed and calm.

Adapted from cosmickids.com

Essential Sites About Addiction

For Parents

aa.org (Alcoholics Anonymous)
cyh.com
futuresofpalmbeach.com
kidshealth.org/teen/your_mind/friends/addictions(teens)
mindfulrp.com (Mindfulness Based Relapse Prevention)
pbskids.org/itsmylife/body/drugabuse
na.org (Narcotics Anonymous)
smartrecovery.org

****

Thank you to cyh.com for resources that were used to create this book.

A Message From The Author

There are lots of people in our world that have addictions. It's easy for everyone to want to have or do something a lot if they really love it!

It's important to NOTICE what we do and say and eat everyday though, to remind ourselves of what we really need. If we listen to our body and brain and pay attention to what it feels like, chances are we will feel a lot better if we give it what it needs.

Its difficult to ALWAYS give it what it needs...sometimes we feel like having chocolate or candy instead of fruit. But, if we try to take care of our body and brain as best as we can and have treats only every once in a while, that's the best we can do and that's just perfect!

Good Luck, Trace:)

A Special Dedication To...
FUTURES of Palm Beach

Futures is a residential treatment center that offers integrated treatment for people struggling with addiction, substance abuse issues and co-occurring medical disorders.

Futures has an All Inclusive Core Program:
24 Hr Medical staff on Duty, Private Bedroom and Private Bath, Medical Detoxification, Medical/Psychosocial/Psychiatric/Dietician Evaluations, Individual/Group/DBT Therapy, Relapse Prevention/Case Management Sessions, Weekend Activities and Programs, Yoga/Meditation Sessions, Family Program. (Please visit website for details about the Premium Program also Available)

The mission at Futures is to create the highest quality addictions and co-occurring disorders program available, combining the most in-depth evidenced-based treatment with a five star level of personal service.

Only at Futures will patients receive a minimum of 12-16 hours of personal treatment sessions each month in a comprehensive introduction to DBT (Dialectical Behavioral Therapy) program that prioritizes the patient and their families.

For more information please visit futuresofpalmbeach.com or call 866.686.5527 to schedule a facility tour

CPSIA information can be obtained
at www.ICGtesting.com
Printed in the USA
LVRC02n0922180418
573904LV00006BA/23

9 781517 523169